UNDERSTANDING BATS

By Kim Williams and Rob Mies

C O N T E N T S

Cover: Hoary bat by Carl R. Sams, II. **Above:** Northern yellow bat by Bruce Montagne.

UNDERSTANDING BATS was produced by the staff of *Bird Watcher's Digest*:
Bill Thompson, III, *Booklet Editor and Booklet Design*; Andy Thompson, *Marketing Director, BWD Press,* Kristen Payson, *Editorial Assistant;* John Metzger, *Production Director;* Jessica Vaughan, *Production Assistant;* Mary Beacom Bowers, *BWD Editorial Consultant.*

Bird Watcher's Digest is published by Pardson Corporation, P.O. Box 110, Marietta, Ohio 45750.
To order additional copies of *UNDERSTANDING BATS*, or our other booklets, *TEACHING KIDS ABOUT BIRDS, ENJOYING BUTTERFLIES MORE, ENJOYING BIRDS MORE, ENJOYING BIRD FEEDING MORE, ENJOYING PURPLE MARTINS MORE, ENJOYING BLUEBIRDS MORE, ENJOYING HUMMINGBIRDS MORE, A GUIDE TO BACKYARD BIRDS,* and *A GUIDE TO BIRD HOMES,* or for *BWD* subscription information, call us toll-free at 1-800-879-2473.
ISBN # 1-880241-12-9.

BAT BASICS

Bats have been misunderstood for centuries.

Bats are among the most fascinating and highly beneficial animals. Although bats have been historically regarded as pests and creatures of bad luck and darkness, today we have a better understanding of these amazing creatures.

Of the thousands of species of mammals, a quarter are bats. Unlike gliding mammals such as the flying squirrel, all bats are capable of true flight. Some of the large fruit bats can even glide like raptors! This ability, plus several other characteristics, led scientists to put the 1,000 species of bats in their own order: Chiroptera. Chiroptera is a Greek word that means "hand-wing." The wing of a bat is very similar to a human hand, with four fingers and a thumb, but a bat's fingers are elongated. Some scientists believe that bats evolved the ability to fly millions of years ago, originating from a shrew-like animal that glided from tree to tree. Though this hypothesis remains unproven, we know that three-million-year-old bat fossils with insects in their stomachs have been found.

Today, there are two main suborders of the order Chiroptera: Megachiroptera and Microchiroptera. The megachiropterans (or megabats) are larger bats, with large eyes and smaller ears in comparison to their body size. The largest megabat, the gigantic flying fox, has a wingspan of almost six feet (about two meters) and can weigh up to two pounds (about one kg)! These bats are fruit eaters and nectar drinkers. Megabats are found only in the Old World tropics—Africa, Asia, Australia, Indonesia, and the southwest Pacific Islands. Because megabats eat fruit and nectar, they do not need to rely on echolocation

JOE MCDONALD

Above: A little brown bat in flight. At right: Mexican free-tailed bats leaving a cave in Texas.

MERLIN D. TUTTLE/ BAT CONSERVATION INTERNATIONAL

(the ability to locate objects in the dark using sound waves) to find a meal; therefore, only one genus, the *Rousettus*, retains its ability to echolocate.

Microchiropterans (or microbats) are smaller, the smallest being the Kitti's hog-nosed bat, which weighs only as much as a dime. This bat has a wingspan of just a few inches and a bumblebee-sized body, and it may be the world's smallest mammal. Microbats have large ears in relation to their eyes, rely on echolocation to find their food, and are found worldwide, except in the Antarctic. Although most microbats eat insects, some specialize in drinking nectar, eating fruit, fish, reptiles, amphibians, mammals, other bats, and yes, even drinking blood.

HOW BATS BENEFIT US

Bats worldwide provide us with numerous benefits. Fruit bats in the tropics pollinate and disperse seeds for more than 80 percent of the tropical rain forest. This is extremely important when we consider how much of the tropics is being destroyed daily. Without many of these bats, we would have reduced regeneration of vital tropical tree species. Fruit bats keep the wild stock of our cultivated fruit trees, such as wild banana, mango, and avocado, viable. If the wild stock were to disappear, scientists would have no unaltered genetic material for these trees. Any disease spreading through the cultivated stock could permanently wipe it out.

Bats emit a series of high-pitched sounds to locate flying prey. This is known as echolocation, and it functions much like radar.

ILLUSTRATION BY JULIE ZICKEFOOSE

In North America, bats are also an important part of our ecosystem. They are an indicator of a healthy environment; the more bats there are in a given area, the lower the amounts of pesticides being used in that area.

Insectivorous bats in North America eat millions of pounds of insects each night. Eating almost their full body weight nightly, they are the major predators of night-flying insects. Farmers have long realized the benefits of bats because bats save them millions of dollars each year by consuming crop pests. If a grown adult human ate as much as a bat did nightly, he or she would have to consume about 150 pounds (68 kg) of french fries, or roughly 50 large pizzas!

ECHOLOCATION

Because bats are most active during the night, how do they find food? North American bats use an amazing technique called echo-location to find their food in the dark of night. A few other mammals, such as whales and dolphins, use echolocation to find their way through murky ocean waters. Although bats can see fairly well, they depend upon echo-location to find their small insect prey. Here's how it works: the bat emits a high frequency sound—much too high for human ears to register—usually through its mouth, and the sound travels until it hits an object. The sound waves then bounce back to the bat's ears. Using this reference point, the bat can get a mental picture of its surroundings. Bats are so adapted to using these sound waves that they can detect a single strand of hair in total darkness. Imagine how advanced this system would have to be for bats to be able to catch and consume 600 to 1,000 mosquito-sized insects in an hour!

REPRODUCTION

Of all bats, a lactating female consumes the greatest number of insects per night. She must eat enough for herself and her pups, which, when born, can weigh up to 25 percent of the mother's weight

AMAZING BAT FACTS

- *In some countries, giant fruit bats are captured and sold at markets for food. This practice is endangering many of these rain forest animals.*
- *The hoary bat is the only mammal indigenous to the Hawaiian islands.*
- *The largest colony of bats, 20 million Brazilian free-tails, is found in central Texas' Bracken Cave.*
- *Millie Hill Mine, located in upper Michigan's Iron Mountain, is thought to contain the largest hibernating colony of bats (almost 1 million).*
- *Microbats' specially adapted vertebrae allow them to bend their necks backward 180 degrees while they are perched.*
- *Male hammer-headed bats have such loud voices that at close range they sound like car alarms! Calling males congregate to form choirs, providing quite a performance in African forests.*

The Parts of a Bat

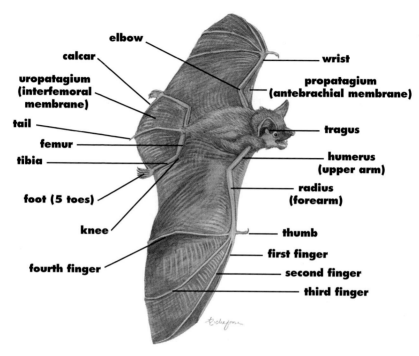

elbow

calcar

wrist

uropatagium (interfemoral membrane)

propatagium (antebrachial membrane)

tail

tragus

femur

tibia

humerus (upper arm)

foot (5 toes)

radius (forearm)

knee

thumb

first finger

fourth finger

second finger

third finger

(as a comparison, a 100-pound [45 kg] woman would have a 25-pound [11 kg] baby!). Most bats have their young in the late spring or early summer, after awakening from hibernation. Many bats will actually mate in the fall, hibernate through the winter, and then become pregnant in the early spring. This is called delayed implantation. Gestation is 30 to 60 days, and females usually have one or two pups per year.

Female bats nurse their young until the young are old enough to fly. At this point, the pups follow their mothers, learning foraging techniques and strategies until they are able to hunt on their own. The female provides supplemental milk until the young are completely independent. The young ones must consume large numbers of insects each night in order to undertake migration and long hibernation through the winter months.

BAT HIBERNATION

Many of North America's most common bats hibernate throughout the winter months. Hibernation is an adaptation bats use to conserve stored energy at a time when their food source is unavailable or severely depleted. During hibernation, bats are very vulnerable to disturbance. Normally, bats will awaken on their own three to four times during the winter to shift positions, but if a disturbance purposely or accidentally awakens them more times than that, many of the bats will use up their stored fat reserves and starve.

Bats hibernate from late October to early April in the northern states, spending much of their lives in a low metabolic state. Because of this, some bats live to age 35, which is quite old considering the small size of most of our bats.

A bat hibernation site is called a hibernaculum. Hibernacula can include old buildings, attics, caves, bridges, tunnels, hollow logs—anywhere a bat can roost, safe from disturbance and harsh weather.

In more southern states, bats will

HELPING BATS IN

The more you vary the habitats within your yard, the greater the diversity of wildlife you will attract. By planting and building to attract bats, you will add beauty and invite other visitors such as butterflies and birds.

WATER

Water attracts insects; insects attract bats. A natural water source is one of the best ways to entice bats and other wildlife to visit your property. Water is important for many insects' first stages of life. Bats naturally forage along streams, creeks, rivers, and over ponds, eating insects as they emerge from the water. Bats skim along the water to drink. If water is not already present on your property, you may wish to construct a small pond. Backyard pond kits are available from most garden centers.

ROOSTING SITES

Planting trees and leaving dead and dying trees standing are wonderful ways to encourage bats to live in your area. Dead trees provide natural habitat for bats, other mammals, and birds. Many colony-roosting bats will use tree cavities and crevices. Good roost sites include the loose, peeling bark of dead trees, hollow trees, and old woodpecker holes. Live trees often provide necessary shelter for solitary bats such as hoary bats, which roost near the trunks and camouflage themselves in the foliage to avoid predators. Piles of logs, shrubs, or mixed woodland make great habitat for all wildlife, including bats.

GARDENS

Bat gardens are another good provider of insects and roosting sites for bats. Flowers that release scent at night, such as sweet rocket, evening primrose, nicotiana, and soapwort, attract night-flying insects that feed on nectar, such as moths. Herbs such as chives, borage, mint, marjoram, and lemon not migrate during winter months; instead they will remain in their day roosts, entering a state of torpor if the temperature drops close to the freezing point. In northern states, bats may do a variety of things during the winter. Colony-roosting bats, such as big brown bats and little brown bats, will try to hibernate in their summer roosts as long as the internal temperature of these roosts does not drop below freezing. If the roosts become too cold, the bats will migrate to areas with caves or mines and spend the winters hibernating there. Solitary roosting bats that live in the North, which can include red bats and hoary bats, avoid hibernating by migrating to southern areas that usually do not have temperatures below freezing. □

YOUR BACKYARD

balm also attract night-flying insects. If you can, leave part of your lawn unmowed during the summer months. This will increase insects whose larvae feed on grasses. Climbing vines such as honeysuckle, ivy, white jasmine, or dogrose will provide roosting sites for solitary bats. Another excellent place to roost is a bat house (see pages 18–21).

LIGHTS

Mercury vapor lights in your yard attract insects, and bats will enjoy these easy meals. Moths are plentiful around such lights, and many solitary bat species such as the red bat will be found there foraging.

BATS & CHEMICALS

Avoid spraying your lawn, trees, and shrubs with pesticides, herbicides, or other toxic chemicals. Insectivorous bats consume mass quantities of insects, and if these insects are sprayed with toxic substances, the bats will ingest them, and will become ill or die. You might need to educate your neighbors and local government about the dangers of spraying and the benefits of protecting bats. For every pest in yards and gardens, there is a naturally occurring predator.

BAT SPECIES PROFILES

North America boasts roughly 40 species of bats, which are divided into three families. All these bats feed on insects, with the exception of three species found in small areas of Arizona, California, and Texas. These three feed on nectar and pollen and are vital to the pollination of many desert plants. Listed below are six species of bats commonly found in North America. Species that use bat houses have a small bat house icon beside their names.

BIG BROWN BAT

(*Eptesicus fuscus*)

Considered the most abundant bat in North America, the big brown bat ranges throughout the northeastern United States as far north as Alaska. Southern Florida and central Texas are the only areas in which this bat is not found. Big brown bats are large, with broad noses; their color varies from russet to dark brown. Big browns are colonial, always choosing to roost with others instead of alone.

Big brown bats seek daytime roosts in dark places and are usually found in buildings and around people. Favored roosts include attics, barns, behind shutters, and under bridges. Many big brown bat colonies have also been reported in bat houses. Big browns emerge from their day roosts at dusk and fly at a height of 20–30 feet (6–9 meters), usually heading toward a stream or river to forage.

There have been many studies involving the feeding habits of the big brown bat. Known to prey upon beetles, wasps, ants, flies, mosquitoes, and many other types of insects, big browns are surprisingly efficient feeders, usually filling their stomachs within an hour. Because many of the insects big brown bats eat are major pests, these bats are considered highly beneficial.

Big brown bats, like most bats, mate in the fall before their long hibernation. Young are born in the spring and early summer. Females might have one or two pups. In Indiana, for example, it is quite common for females to give birth to twins. The newborns hang tightly to

BIG BROWN BAT
SIZE: Head to toe about 3.5 inches (9cm).
WINGSPAN: 13–14 inches.
COLOR: Light to dark brown.
IDENTIFYING ON THE WING: Large size and steady flight make it recognizable in flight.
OTHER: Females weigh slightly more than males. Ears small.

BRUCE MONTAGNE

BAT MAPS BY SUSAN EUGSTER/PUBLICATION DESIGN, INC.

their mothers during the day, cradled beneath the wing membranes. When the mothers fly from the roost in the evening to begin foraging, they leave their pups in the roost. If the pups are very young, the mothers leave early in the evening to forage for insects close by, returning frequently to check on their newborns. Occasionally, young bats may fall out of the roost, and although some die, many are picked up and cared for by their mothers.

Big brown bats will choose to hibernate in any structure in which the temperature does not drop below freezing. Favored hibernacula include houses, barns, and garages. If roost temperatures drop below freezing, the bats will migrate to an area that has caves or mines and hibernate there, escaping subfreezing temperatures. Young bats learn this

behavior from their mothers.

Big brown bats are the most common bats seen in backyards and are the most regular users of bat houses in the North.

LITTLE BROWN BAT
(*Myotis lucifigus*)

At first glance, little brown bats look like big browns. However, little brown bats are much smaller, and their color ranges from pale tan to reddish or dark brown. Little browns are found throughout northern North America, as far north as Alaska. Like big brown bats, little browns are colonial.

During summer months, this species is found mostly in buildings, choosing a hot attic if at all possible. They have also been found behind shutters and in bat houses. Colonies of little brown bats are most often

JOE MCDONALD

LITTLE BROWN BAT

SIZE: Head to toe about 2 inches (5cm).
WINGSPAN: 9–10 inches.
COLOR: Tan to dark brown. Glossy fur.
IDENTIFYING ON THE WING: Flight is swift
and erratic.
OTHER: Long hairs on toes. Large feet.

located near a lake, stream, or other body of water.

Little brown bats roost by day and forage by night. At dusk, they emerge from the roost and head for water, hunting a few feet above the water for most of the evening. The evening feeding is alternated with periods of rest so that the bats can digest their food. If water is not nearby, little brown bats will feed among trees, or over lawns, pastures, or streets near their roost. Here they forage at heights of 10–20 feet (3–6 meters). Favorite food sources include gnats, wasps, beetles, and moths. Bats use their interfemoral (tail) membrane or a wing membrane to catch insects, and then grasp them with their mouths. The flight pattern of the little brown bat is erratic, sometimes attaining speeds of up to 22 mph

(35 km per hour).

Little brown bats have the same hibernating behavior as big browns. Colonies will break up in the early fall and shift to a hibernaculum. They will occasionally hibernate in structures such as houses, garages, and barns, but they are more likely to congregate in caves or mines to spend the winter. They will sometimes migrate as far as 170 miles (275 km) to get to their hibernating areas. The bats will spend roughly five months in hibernation, surviving solely on their fat reserves.

RED BAT
(*Lasiurus borealis*)

The red bat is one of North America's most beautiful bats. Its color ranges from bright orange to yellow-brown, with the males in the

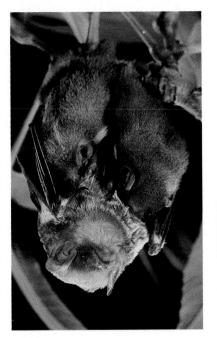

MERLIN D. TUTTLE/ BAT CONSERVATION INTERNATIONAL

RED BAT

SIZE: Head to toe about 3.5 inches (9cm).
WINGSPAN: 11–13 inches.
COLOR: Bright orange to yellow-brown.
IDENTIFYING ON THE WING: Long, pointed
wings; swift flight at treetop level.
OTHER: Short, round ears. Furred tail.

eastern parts of the range a much more vibrant shade of orange than the females. This is one of the only bat species to exhibit this male/female color differentiation, or sexual dimorphism, which is common among bird species. The long tail and interfemoral membrane make this bat easily recognizable. The interfemoral membrane is heavily furred, and in flight the tail extends straight out behind the bat.

Red bats are most abundant in the Midwest and east central states. They are found especially in woodlands and prairies. They are also found in California, Arizona, and Utah.

Red bats are solitary roosting bats, except during the pup-raising season when mother and pups roost together. Red bats roost in the foliage of trees, where they choose the stem of a leaf to hang on. Hanging in a tree by one foot, a red bat looks just like a dead leaf.

Red bats emerge early in the evening and are seen at treetop level in swift flight. They then descend and feed below treetop level. Observing these bats in flight is not as tricky as it may seem. Look for long, pointed wings and swift flight [up to 40 mph (64km)] at low levels. Red bats will forage over the same territory nightly, and occasionally you can see one or two scouting for insects around street lights in urban areas.

Red bats forage for crickets, flies, bugs, beetles, cicadas, and many other types of insects. It is interesting that terrestrial crickets are part of these bats' diets. This seems to suggest that they take some of their food from the ground.

BRUCE MONTAGNE

HOARY BAT
SIZE: Head to toe about 4.5 inches (11cm).
WINGSPAN: 15–16 inches.
COLOR: Dark gray frosted with white; heavily furred.
IDENTIFYING ON THE WING: Large, swift bat that flies in direct path.
OTHER: Ears short, rounded.

In late summer and early fall, red bats have been known to congregate at dusk around corncribs to feed upon grain moths. This demonstrates how red bats can be highly beneficial to farmers.

Red bats migrate to warm climates, where they spend the winter hanging from trees, occasionally going into a state of torpor in much the same manner as hummingbirds.

HOARY BAT
(*Lasiurus cinereus*)

Hoary bats are among the largest bats found in North America. They are rare throughout most of eastern North America, but become more common in the open prairies. The hoary bat is common in southern California, Arizona, and New Mexico. Although rare in some states, the hoary bat is the most widespread of all North American bats, found in 49 states, including Hawaii. They have not yet been reported in Alaska.

The hoary bat is a large, dark-colored, heavily furred bat, with the interfemoral membrane completely furred. The tips of the hoary bat's fur are white, giving the bat a frosted or hoary look.

The flight style of the hoary bat is swift and direct. Emerging late in the evening, the bats often emit audible chattering while in flight. This chattering is their way of communicating with each other, and is not the same as the sounds they emit for echolocation.

Like red bats, hoary bats are solitary by nature, roosting with other bats only when they have young ones. They stay relatively well concealed in the foliage of

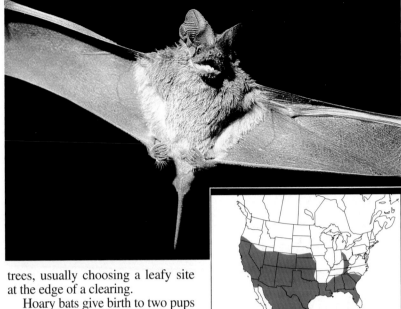

trees, usually choosing a leafy site at the edge of a clearing.

Hoary bats give birth to two pups each summer. Pups cling to their mother throughout the day; at night, she leaves them clinging to a twig or branch as she forages.

Hoary bats fly a great distance when migrating to a warmer climate. Like migratory birds, the bats move in waves, sometimes following rivers and lake shores to get to their southern wintering grounds. They stay in these southern areas until spring, when they migrate back north and the females give birth.

Not much is known about the hoary bat's feeding behavior. Scientists have reported these bats chasing moths and found insects and mosquitoes in the stomachs of some.

BRAZILIAN FREE-TAILED BAT

(*Tadarida brasiliensis*)

The Brazilian free-tailed bat is a small brown bat with long wings. The lower half of its tail is free from the interfemoral membrane, hence the name free-tailed. Brazilian free-

BRAZILIAN FREE-TAILED BAT
SIZE: Head to toe about 3.5 inches (9cm).
WINGSPAN: 11–13 inches.
COLOR: Dark grayish-brown.
IDENTIFYING ON THE WING: Long, narrow wings; straight, rapid flight in groups 15-20 feet (5-6 meters) above ground.
OTHER: End of tail free from membrane. Large ears.

tailed bats are found throughout the southern United States and north into a small area of Oregon. Individuals have been found as far north as southern Ohio.

These bats hang in large clusters, forming the largest colonies in the world. These colonies are usually found in caves, buildings, and bat houses. Great flights of these bats can be observed at Carlsbad Caverns, New Mexico, in summer, and even larger colonies occur in Arizona, Texas, and Mexico. Each night in summer, hundreds of people

SILVER-HAIRED BAT
SIZE: Head to toe about 3 inches (8cm).
WINGSPAN: 11–12 inches.
COLOR: Black. Hair-tips silver.
IDENTIFYING ON THE WING: Low-flying, slow flight early in evening.
OTHER: Tail membrane is lightly furred.

ROB SIMPSON

gather to sit on the banks of the Colorado River in Austin, Texas, to watch the emergence of millions of these bats from under the Congress Avenue Bridge where they roost. The residents of Austin greatly appreciate the help the bats give them in controlling insect pests.

Freetails usually leave their roosts in groups, especially from caves where millions live. These groups of a few to dozens of bats form upward-spiraling clusters. When they are 50–100 feet (15–30 meters) above the roost, the group moves laterally. The flights ascend to approximately 100 feet (30 meters); the bats then break off into small groups that fly off in different directions. The groups then forage at 15–30 feet (5–9 meters) above the ground for the rest of the evening.

The large colonies of Brazilian free-tailed bats in which expectant females congregate are called nursery colonies. A single pup is born each year. During the day, the pups hang together in large masses away from the mothers. The mother bats will crawl to their young and nurse them several times a day. When they go out to forage for insects, the mothers leave the young ones in the roost.

Brazilian free-tailed bats feed primarily on small moths. Most bats catch insects using their inter-femoral membrane; the membrane of free-tailed bats, however, does not extend more than halfway to the tail. This suggests that these bats catch insects in their mouths. Their long, narrow wings, small size, and straight, rapid flight are important field marks.

Brazilian free-tailed bats hibernate in great numbers during the winter. They usually choose caves, bridges, or other structures in southern states, dispersing to form nursery colonies in the spring. In the western parts of their range, however, they either migrate south or remain, going torpid if necessary.

SILVER-HAIRED BAT

(*Lasionycteris noctivagans*)

Silver-haired bats are medium-sized bats that have black hair with silver tips. Their range is from Alaska throughout most of the United States, except Florida; however, their distribution is uneven. Found in greatest abundance in the northern Rockies, in parts of New England, and New York, they migrate in May through Arizona, New Mexico, and Illinois. In April the bats are found in larger numbers in Kentucky and Tennessee.

Silver-haired bats migrate in groups, and bird banders have reported cases where these bats have been captured in mist-nets along with birds. Silver-haired bats migrate to warmer climates, where they hibernate in trees or in woodpiles during the winter.

A typical roost for silver-haired bats is behind the loose bark of trees. Some silver-haireds have also been found in old woodpecker holes and hanging from birds' nests. During fall migration, these bats may be found in buildings or piles of lumber.

Silver-haired bats emerge earlier in the evening than most bats and fly very low to the ground. Their flight is slow and leisurely, ranging from almost ground level to about 20 feet (6 meters) above ground. Their favorite foraging grounds are woodland ponds and streams, and they habitually follow the same hunting pattern each night. Usually solitary, silver-haired bats may occasionally be found in pairs, and sometimes in groups of three or four.

MORE ABOUT BATS

You may find more information on bat identification and range maps in other literature. Keep in mind, however, that there is not much published on bats, and you may need to search a while to find it. *Bats of America* by Roger Barbour and Wayne Davis is an excellent reference book that outlines and gives great detail on every bat species found in North America. Although a highly recommended book, it was published in 1969; much new information on bats is not included. *Walker's Bats of the World* by Ronald Nowak is a comprehensive guide to bats worldwide. *America's Neighborhood Bats* by Merlin Tuttle describes many common bats of the United States; this book is fairly easy to find in book stores and libraries. *Bats* by M. Brock Fenton is another excellent reference that is in print and available through most bookstores. □

VAMPIRE BATS!

There are three species of vampire bats, all found in Central and South America. Vampire bats are actually quite small, contrary to their movie portrayal. These bats are very shy, but their diets include small amounts of blood. People used to be terrified of vampire bats. Today, scientists understand the great potential vampire bats offer to medical research. For example, vampire bat saliva is being tested as an anticoagulant for heart patients.

BATS & BAT HOUSES

Will bats use bat houses?

Research on the roosting preferences of bats has lead to new bat house designs and guidelines for house placement. For specific information on bat house design, see the inside back cover of this booklet.

BRUCE MONTAGNE

In the United States and around the world, natural bat habitat is diminishing quickly. Bat houses help bats by providing human-made roosting space when natural habitat is scarce. Bat houses are usually made of wood and simulate natural roosting habitats.

Not all bat species will use bat houses. Those species that are solitary roosters (such as the hoary bat, red bat, and silver-haired bat) are less likely to use a bat house. It is the colony-roosting bats (such as little brown and big brown bats, Brazilian free-tailed bats, and others) that are the most likely to take advantage of the housing we can provide. The following suggestions will help you make your site as attractive as possible to bats.

BAT HOUSE DESIGN

A bat house built to the correct specifications and placed appropriately will greatly increase your chance of attracting bats.

Bats are warm-blooded animals, but they can maintain a body temperature similar to their surroundings. As a result, they expend less energy when resting. The fact that bats are able to monitor their own temperatures makes the design of a bat house very important. If bat houses do not offer warmer and cooler sections, the bats can actually become too cold and die. Recently researched models take into consideration the temperature variation that bats require.

New bat houses are designed to be more temperature efficient, offering bats long chambers that provide a variety of roost temperatures. The inside of the bat house contains a ceiling that traps heat and provides extra warmth. This is especially important on cool days, when the bats can crawl to the top of the bat house to keep warm. On hot days, a ventilation slit near the bottom of the house allows the bats to move lower to keep themselves from overheating.

Even one bat house can do much good. According to the University of Florida, a small bat house can house about 100 bats, while a multi-chamber bat house can accommodate as many as 300.

In addition to longer chambers, bats prefer narrower chambers. Years of research have shown that narrow chambers protect a bat colony from the threat of predation. In older designs, wide (greater than one inch) open chambers, coupled with short structures made the bats easy prey for animals such as blue jays, raccoons, or household cats. Bat houses are now designed with narrow openings ($^3/_4$" to 1" wide) to protect them from predators.

New designs also offer a landing platform that extends below the entrance of the house. Landing areas are important for easy access, especially for young bats. Young bats, known as pups, that are just fledged may have coordination problems, making it difficult for them to land on or near a roost. Landing platforms make these maneuvers much easier. Houses that offer a grooved, rough, or plastic-mesh area from the landing platform to the top of the house provide easy footing for clumsy pups. Bat houses that have been unoccupied for years can be made more attractive to bats by the addition of landing areas below the house entrances.

More than 20,000 Brazilian free-tailed bats roost in the bat house on the University of Florida's main campus. The bat house project began as an alternative to the bats' living in the football stadium.

CHECKING FOR BATS

Inspecting your bat house at least once a week is recommended so that you can track whether or not your house is occupied. Bats will switch roosts periodically throughout the summer; reasons for switching vary, and research is being conducted to try to find some answers. Meanwhile, there are a number of procedures you can use to check your bat house for occupants. One way is to look under the house or on the landing area for guano (bat droppings). This indicates that bats are either in the house now or have used it in the past. Another way to check is to shine a strong flashlight up into the house and look. You don't want to do this more than once a week, however, because frequent disturbance may cause the colony to abandon the roost. The best way to check for bats is to view them leaving the house around sunset. Most bats will emerge within a half-hour after sunset. This is the time to record data about the bats living in your bat house.

Bats that commonly occupy bat houses include Brazilian free-tailed bats in the South, pallid bats in the West, little brown bats in the North, eastern pipistrelles in the East, and big brown bats throughout North America. Some of the other 40 North American and Canadian bat species have been reported using bat houses, but these are rare occurrences.

HOUSE PLACEMENT

Researchers now know much more about placement requirements for bat houses. Bat houses should be placed on a tree, pole, house, barn, garage, or any other structure that is at least 15 feet tall. The higher the bat house is placed, the better your chances of attracting bats. When erecting a bat house, you should keep in mind that houses attached to trees usually attract bats one season later than houses placed on structures or poles, probably because the tree canopy conceals the houses. Two bat houses placed back to back on a pole offer the greatest chance of attracting bats.

Houses should be positioned so that they face south or southeast, preferably so that they get morning sunlight. In northern states, the bat houses should receive at least six hours of direct sunlight daily. Remember, bats like their houses very warm, especially those bats in nursery colonies. If you live in a northern state, you can paint the exterior of your bat house black to maximize the house's heat absorption. Just make sure to use non-toxic paint, and never paint the inside of the house. If you live in a warmer southern location, use trial and error to find the perfect spot for your bat houses. In southern Florida, some houses placed in direct sunlight have attracted bats, while others placed in shady areas have had success as well. Your best bet would be to erect several bat houses in a variety of locations.

If you are interested in more detailed bat house plans, or specific temperature requirements of those bats commonly found in your area, please contact the Organization for Bat Conservation (see page 32).

ATTRACTING BATS

Besides putting up bat houses, a number of other methods will entice bats to live on your property. Planting and building to attract bats will add beauty to your yard and invite other visitors such as butterflies and birds. Ponds or other water sources attract insects and other creatures. Bats may also drink and forage for insects over a source of water. Books on wildlife gardening often have plans for pond construction.

In addition to the bat attraction hints on pages 8 and 9, you can encourage bats by varying your yard's habitat. Offer chemical-free habitat. Bats and other wildlife will appreciate it. □

HOW TO GET INVOLVED IN A BACKYARD BAT HOUSE STUDY

The Organization for Bat Conservation (OBC) is seeking reports of bats using bat houses. If bats are using a bat house on your property, you can contribute important data that can help in bat conservation. Send a self-addressed envelope to the OBC (address on page 32) to receive a site registration form. Data reported from across the continent will be analyzed, and the results will be published in scientific journals. This information is vital to finding the most appropriate bat house sites for various species of bats. Your contribution will help bat conservation efforts throughout North America.—*Rob Mies and Kim Williams*

Several hundred bats may crowd into a single bat house. This bat house is full of Brazilian free-tailed bats.

BATS AND

Many people are terrified of bats. For centuries bats have been vilified by human beings. Their poor image stems from the fact that they are nocturnal, waking and emerging at night to forage. Night and darkness have been closely associated with evil and death for centuries, and human beings have been, and still are, superstitious about any animal that forages during the night hours. Owls, cats, snakes, and bats have all therefore had a negative, menacing image. This image has persisted, even though we now have the technology to light up the night.

It is interesting that in countries in which bats are diurnal (active during the day), bats are regarded as a sign of happiness, and seeing them is considered lucky.

MYTHS ABOUT BATS

Bad impressions about bats are often reinforced by the media and the movie industry. News reports often cover unusual, dangerous, or exciting stories. Movies often exaggerate events or simply invent them to create compelling stories. Because the only exposure many people have had to bats comes from these sources, bats continue to have a negative image.

The truth is that bats do not terrorize people any more than people terrorize bats. True, a bat will occasionally accidentally fly into a home, but if everyone involved remains calm, opens up windows and doors, and then sits quietly, the bat will quickly orient itself and fly back outside. If people are running around in a panic, yelling and swatting at the bat, it too will panic and be unable to find its way out. Try to remember that being caught in a human's house is traumatic for a bat. We are very large and frightening to a small creature.

Another way to get a bat out of your house is to wait until the bat lands, carefully place a coffee can over it, slide a piece of cardboard under the open end of the can, scoop up the bat and take it outside. You can also throw a towel or blanket over the bat and take it outside.

SICK OR INJURED BATS

Occasionally you may find a sick or injured bat lying on the ground. In this case, the best thing to do is to use a heavy glove and place the bat on a tree out of harm's way. There are bat rehabilitation centers throughout North America. For information on rehabilitation centers in your state, please call the Organization for Bat Conservation.

HUMANS

The myth that all bats have rabies and that all bats carry the rabies virus persists. Actually, very few bats get the rabies virus, and most of these bats are never seen by people. But because rabies is such a dangerous disease, one that is fatal without proper treatment, and because outbreaks of it are relatively rare, it is always given serious attention by the media. However, just as a single raccoon with rabies does not mean that all raccoons have

Educational programs give people of all ages new and accurate information about bats.

rabies, a single bat with rabies does not indicate that all bats have rabies.

In fact, most statistics you hear on the number of rabid bats are inaccurate or are inaccurately interpreted. For example, if in one year a state wildlife agency receives 10 bats to be tested for rabies—

keeping in mind, these are bats that were probably sick and were found on the ground—and seven of these 10 bats test positive for the rabies virus, the media report that 70 percent of all bats tested that year were rabies positive. This is obviously a skewed statistic. Healthy bat populations are rarely tested, and when they have been, the results show that .5 percent of the bats tested positive for rabies, a rate of occurrence no higher than that for other mammals.

More people die every year from dog attacks or from hitting deer on the road than from rabies. Just remember, never handle any ill or injured wild animal without taking protective measures, and you will not have to worry about rabies. This includes playing with, or allowing children to play with, wild animals. If you have children, teach them at an early age to respect wildlife. Wild animals should be enjoyed from a distance and not touched.

EVICTING AND EXCLUDING BATS

Although many people now understand the benefits of allowing bats to roost near their homes, most are still not ready to accept bats living in their attics. OBC gets hundreds of calls each year requesting advice on bat eviction. Some people want to know if shining a bright light into an attic or other roosting spot will encourage bats to leave. While this might work for solitary roosting bats, it will not be effective with bat colonies. Evicting a colony of bats is not very difficult, but the exclusion process that follows an eviction is time-consuming.

Rather than physically forcing bats to leave their roost (the common definition of eviction), simply wait until they leave at dusk to do their usual nightly foraging. Then you can prevent them from returning to their roost by doing some very simple exclusion procedures. Just remember that in most of northern North America, you should not do bat exclusions during the months of June, July, or August. At these times there will be flightless young in the roost. If you only exclude the mothers, the pups will be trapped inside and will starve. Not only is this cruel, but it will also leave a very bad odor in your house. Exclusions are best done in early spring before the pups are born or in late fall after the young are already on the wing.

Here's how to do a bat exclusion. Each evening, watch your house in various locations to find out exactly where the bats are entering and exiting. You may want to enlist the help of a friend to speed this process. Chances are, you will observe the bats using more than one opening. Next to or near the opening(s), temporarily install a bat house. It is important to get the bat house as close as possible to the opening so that the bats can see it as they exit and enter. Leave the bat house or houses in place for three to four days. You want the bats to get used to the bat house, and some may even move in before the exclusion.

After you have established the bats' entrance and exit points and gotten them accustomed to the new bat house(s), you are ready for the next step. Shape a piece of light hardware cloth or wire screening into a cylinder and place it over the

BRUCE MONTAGNE

bats' exit from your dwelling, taping the edges securely to the walls. This tube will allow the bats to leave. When they return, the bats do not know to reenter the end of the cylinder, and thus they are excluded from the dwelling.

Alternatively, you can tape a square piece of screen or hardware cloth to the house on three sides (see photograph above). Bats can easily exit the house, but cannot crawl under the wire cloth to get back in.

Leave this excluder in place for about a week. With any luck, by this time, all the bats will have moved from your house into the bat house.

BAT GUANO

Many people have reservations about the effects of bat droppings, or guano. Bat guano, unless encountered in hot, humid caves where millions of bats reside, is harmless. As a matter of fact, it makes excellent fertilizer when sprinkled on gardens.

In large quantities, and in arid conditions, a fungus may grow on bat guano. If this fungus is disturbed, the spores erupt and may be inhaled by humans. This can cause flulike symptoms called histoplasmosis. Many pigeon keepers and chicken farmers must also be careful about contracting this disease. It is worth noting, however, that 70 percent of all people living in the Ohio River Valley have at some time been exposed to histoplasmosis because of migrating flocks of blackbirds and starlings, which can also spread this illness. If you need to be in a hot attic with hundreds of bats and large amounts of bat guano, use a high quality HEPA face mask to filter out the fungus spores.

Beside being great fertilizer, bat guano has had other uses. During the War of 1812 and again during the American Civil War, bat guano mined from caves was an important component of gun powder. Some of these caves were so important that guards were stationed at the entrances to keep enemies away. Bats were also part of a secret plan against the Japanese during World War II. Brazilian free-tailed bats were to have small bombs attached to their backs. The bats would then be dropped from an airplane over Japanese cities in a parachuted cage. At a specific time, the cage would open and the bats would fly out and take up residence in buildings of the cities. The plan intended for the bats to groom themselves, detaching the bombs and thus blowing up the building. This plan was abandoned, which was fortunate for more than the bats! □

QUESTIONS

Everywhere we travel in North America, people have plenty of questions about bats. Part of our mission is to educate society about bats, so we view these questions as an opportunity both to teach people about bats and to do a service to bats. The more people understand about bats, the more likely they are to help them.

These questions are among those we are asked most often:

Q: What good are bats?

Bats provide humans with many benefits. Microbats eat millions of pounds of insects nightly, saving farmers millions of dollars in pesticides, and saving the average home owner a great deal of money in insect repellent and electricity for running expensive bug zappers. Because microbats mate in the fall but do not become pregnant until spring, scientists have used certain bat hormones for birth control studies. Doctors have used the advanced sonar system in bats for work with the blind. Vampire bat saliva has been used in many studies to treat heart problems. Along with megabats, microbats that live in the tropics and eat fruit and drink nectar provide the environment with a never-ending supply of genetic diversity, regen-eration of rain forest trees, and the pollination of key plant species. Without these bats, we might never see our tropical rain forests regenerate.

Q: How can I help bats?

Two main problems exist that threaten the future of bats: human attitudes toward bats and habitat destruction. Effective protection of bats will involve a few simple steps. First, people need to be educated about bats to change their attitudes. Not only can you tell others about the benefits and uniqueness of bats, but you can also dispel myths and make it clear that bats are not dangerous. Second, you can plan conservation projects. Finally, you can create an appreciation of natural habitat and its importance to the survival of bats and other living things. Bats not only eat tons of insects every night, but they also pollinate plants, disperse seeds, and provide food for natural predators. By teaching others about bats, you can help protect bats and their natural habitat.

Q: Are there bat clubs or organizations to help bats?

There are several bat organizations that protect bats and their habitats (see list on page 32). You

ABOUT BATS

ROB SIMPSON

can also start a bat education club in your area. You and others who are interested in bats can educate people about bats and their benefits. If you are interested in starting a bat education club, please write to the OBC.

Q: Is there any place where bats do not live?

Bats do not live in Antarctica, where the weather is too cold.

Q: Do bats make good pets?

No, bats do not make good pets, any more than a wild bird makes a

Vampire bats do drink blood. In fact, their teeth and digestive systems are specially adapted to this diet. These bats, native to Central and South America, consume harmless amounts of blood from native birds, mammals, and domestic livestock.

good pet. Bats are meant to be wild creatures and have not become domesticated like dogs and cats. A bat in captivity is very unhappy, stressed to its limit, and probably will not live out its entire lifespan. It is illegal to keep bats as pets.

Northern yellow bats are found in southern Florida, where they commonly roost in Spanish moss.

Q: How long do bats live?

Different species of bats live different lengths of time. The smaller microbats that hibernate through the winter can live as long as 35 years. That is relatively long considering their small size. Larger bats found in the tropics tend not to live as long, probably because they do not hibernate. These bats can live from 15 to 25 years.

Q: Why do bats hang upside down?

Scientists from all over the world have speculated about this. It is now believed that bats adapted to living in caves as they evolved. In caves there are no branches or areas in which to sit upright, so bats were forced to hang upside down. If they were to hang by their thumbs, which appears possible at first glance, they would not be able to take off or groom themselves. Another advantage to hanging upside down is that many bats can fit together in a tight cluster, thus conserving body heat. This is especially beneficial to bats during colder periods in winter when they hibernate.

Q: When do bats hibernate?

This depends on the species of bat and the climate in which the bat lives. In southern climes, some bats do not hibernate at all; they simply go into a daily torpor in the winter.

BRUCE MONTAGNE

Torpor is a response bats have to cooler temperatures. They are able to drop their body temperature close to the external air temperature, thus saving energy. In northern climes, colony-roosting bats (e.g., big browns, little browns, and evening bats) begin their hibernation as early as October if the weather is cold. Our solitary-roosting bats—red bats and hoary bats—can withstand cooler temperatures and are sometimes found in more northern areas until November or early December. Solitary roosting bats are able to wrap their fully furred interfemoral membrane (the tail membrane) tightly around themselves for extra warmth.

Natural roosting sites for bats are becoming more and more scarce. Bat houses can help alleviate this scarcity.

Q: Can bats see?

Yes, all bats can see relatively well, some much better than others. Microbats, which rely on echolocation, can see well during the day, and about as well as you and I at night. Microbats are thought to be color-blind. The megabats, which eat fruit or drink nectar from flowers, have exceptionally good color eyesight, similar to the vision of an owl or cat at night. Most megabats lack the ability to echolocate, and therefore rely totally on their eyesight when foraging for fruit.

Q: Are bats endangered?

Around the world there are many species of bats that are threatened and endangered, although the reasons for this are varied. Foremost is the lack of suitable roosting habitat. As humans encroach on bat habitat, we tend to view bats as pests and remove them. Millions upon millions of bats are killed this way every year. Another problem bats have is indiscriminate human persecution. Many times, when people find bat roosts they purposely destroy the roosts or bats because of an uninformed fear of these harmless mammals or the disease they are presumed to carry.

In North America we have many endangered species of bats. One example is the Indiana bat (*Myotis sodalis*). Indiana bats have never been found in great numbers, but their population has declined sharply in recent years. Forty years ago, there were several caves and mines in some eastern states that housed hundreds of Indiana bats. Now few bats of this species are found in this area. During the 1950s, Indiana bats nearly disappeared in West Virginia, Indiana, and Illinois, and populations in Missouri have also been depleted. This sharp decline was caused by human interference. The destruction of wetland areas in which bats raise their young, and the closing up of hibernacula (caves and mines) are the main causes. The Organization for Bat Conservation is devoted to the ecological study of this federally endangered bat. For more information, please refer to the OBC's publication titled "Summer Roosts of the Endangered Indiana Bat (*Myotis sodalis*) on the Northern Edge of Its Range."

Q: How many types of bats live in North America?

There are roughly 40 different species of bats in North America. These 40 species represent three families. Throughout the world there are about 1,000 different species of bats. The greatest diversity is found in the tropical rain forests.

If a bat gets caught in your house, open the doors and windows and calmly sit down. The bat will use echolocation to find its way out.

Q: What is the biggest bat in the world and what is the smallest?

The largest bat in the world is a megabat called the gigantic flying fox, found in Pakistan, India, Nepal, and on islands in the Indian Ocean. This bat has a wingspan of 5–6 feet (about 2 meters)! The principle food source of the gigantic flying fox is fruit, which it chews up, swallowing the juice and spitting out the pulp and seeds. This seed dispersion helps to reforest vast areas of the tropics.

Because this bat eats fruit, orchard farmers in third-world countries are very intolerant of it. The bats, however, have very little choice, with their natural food source depleted through deforestation. In the past 10 or so years, populations of these bats have seriously declined. Reasons include loss of habitat, eradication by farmers, and excessive hunting of them for meat.

The smallest bat in the world—and perhaps the smallest mammal in the world—is the Kitti's hog-nosed bat. This bat is very rare. About the size of a large bumblebee, it has a weight of less than 1 ounce (about 2 grams). The Kitti's hog-nosed bat forages for insects around the canopy of bamboo and teak trees in Thailand.

Q: Don't all bats have rabies?

No, not all bats have rabies, just as not all rabbits, raccoons, or foxes have rabies. Rabies is a serious virus that affects the brain tissue of mammals, and although it is true that bats can get rabies, they are not carriers of the virus. If you see a bat or any other wild animal lying on the ground, not trying to get away from humans or otherwise acting strangely, call your local department of natural resources or other state wildlife agency and ask them to help you take care of the problem. If you are far from a telephone, it is best to leave the animal alone and let nature take its course.

Q: Why are there bats in my attic?

To a bat, a dark, warm attic is just like a natural cave. Luckily for us, there are easy ways to evict bats and to provide a housing alternative for them (see page 24).

Q: What is the quickest way to get a bat out of my house?

If you have a bat flying around inside your house, the easiest and quickest way to get it out is to open a door or window and calmly sit down to watch and wait for the bat to fly out. You do not have to turn off the lights. If this does not work, throw a soft towel or blanket over the bat and gently place it outside. Remember, bats are small and fragile creatures; they are not in your house to frighten or harm you in any way. They are probably just as scared as you, if not more. Using a tennis racket or any other object to harm a bat is not necessary.

Q: Do bat houses really work?

Bat houses have long been a subject of controversy. Do they work? Is there any benefit to putting one up? Is there any disadvantage to putting one up?

The new style bat houses (see section on bat houses) work extremely well. By putting up a bat house, you are providing a much-needed home for bats. Every day thousands of bats are being evicted from their roosts and homes. Natural habitat for bats is becoming more and more scarce. Your bat house will give a home to bats that would otherwise quickly die if they could not find a suitable place to live. The bats that live in your bat house are doing you a tremendous favor: they are eating thousands of insects nightly during warm weather.

Q: I would like to build my own bat house or buy one. What dimensions and materials are the most attractive to bats?

A bat house should resemble the peeling bark of a dead tree: long, thin, and rough. We suggest using untreated cedar or exterior plywood. Minimum size should be 2' tall x 15" wide x 3" deep (depending on how many interior chambers you want). The entrance to the chambers needs to be about ³/₄" wide. The house should be rough inside or covered with mesh on which the bats can hang. A landing area that extends at least five inches beneath the entrance is also necessary.

Q: If I put up a bat house, will the bats interfere with my bird feeder?

No. Bats do not compete with birds, either for space or food. Bats and birds come out at different times to forage. Birds are out from sunrise to sunset, while bats are out from sunset to sunrise. Also, bats are not aggressive feeders and would not drive away birds even if they were out during the day. Besides, North American bats don't eat bird seed.

Q: Will bats come back to the same bat house every year?

Yes. Once a colony of bats has found your bat house, they will use that same house every year. If you live in a northern climate where bats hibernate, the bats will leave the bat house during the winter months and hibernate and will return to your bat house in the spring to raise their young.

Q: If I put up a bat house near my home, will bats move into my atttic?

No. Bats attracted to your bat house will not automatically move into your attic. Bats prefer to roost in their own house (especially in the type of bat houses described elsewhere in this book), and some people have actually reported colonies of bats moving from attics into bat houses once the houses were available. □

FOR MORE INFORMATION

Bat conservation organizations play an important role in the education of the general public, governmental agencies, and private corporations. These organizations present educational programs, offer adopt-a-bat projects, and provide opportunities to get involved with current bat research. Many research projects center around the ever-growing number of threatened or endangered bats worldwide. Results from such projects encourage local governments to take action to save their declining bat populations.

If you are interested in learning more, write to the following national and international organizations:

CARL R. SAMS, II

The Organization for Bat Conservation
The OBC provides educational programs, material, and advice about bats. Members receive the quarterly *Bat Conservation Journal*, discounts on bat-related gifts, and a chance to join various projects. Volunteer opportunities in bat research, conservation, and public education are available.

2300 Epley Road
Williamston, Michigan 48895
E-mail: obcbats@aol.com
(517) 655-9200

Bat Conservation International, Inc.
Educational publications and programs, books about bats, bat houses, and other items are available from BCI, Inc., a non-profit membership organization. Members receive the quarterly publication, *Bats*, with contributions by leading experts who write clearly for non-scientists. The organization's purpose is to document and publicize the value and conservation needs of bats, to promote conservation and research projects, and to assist with management initiatives worldwide.

P.O. Box 162603
Austin, Texas 78716-2693
(512) 327-9721

Bat Conservation Society of Canada
P.O. Box 56042
Airways Postal Outlet
Calgary, Alberta, Canada T2E 8K5
E-mail: BCSC@cadvision.com